T0170645

RUN RIOT

Dagger Editions, an imprint of Caitlin Press Inc.
8100 Alderwood Road,
Halfmoon Bay, BC V0N 1Y1
www.daggereditions.com
www.caitlin-press.com

Cover and text design by Sarah Corsie
Cover image "For My Part I Know Nothing With Any Certainty but the Sight of the Stars Makes Me Dream III" by Kari Kristensen
Printed in Canada

Caitlin Press Inc. acknowledges financial support from the Government of Canada and the Canada Council for the Arts, and the Province of British Columbia through the British Columbia Arts Council and the Book Publisher's Tax Credit.

Library and Archives Canada Cataloguing in Publication

Run riot : ninety poems in ninety days / poems by Ash Winters.
Winters, Ash, 1988– author.
Canadiana 20200375687 | ISBN 9781773860541 (softcover)
LCC PS8645.I5743 R86 2021 | DDC C811/.6—dc23

Run Riot

Ninety Poems in Ninety Days

by Ash Winters

Dagger Editions 2021

For Duncan and Sarah-Jane

Tiptoe me back to decent
like it is a place I have been before
old versions of myself dance
confused with themselves
waltz and a hula
trying to hold hands
trying to pretend they are at the same party
trying to pretend that they came with someone
only place I know where they ask you to think about
how you feel about what you think
Sure

Ride out my mechanical bull feelings
that's right they are not real
pretend I am not in the racetrack dirt floor stadium of my mind
but that bull just looked at me with all the self-hate of thirty years
Of course I won't die if I fall
well?
I have a good chance of dodging the hoof to the head
mostly though don't fall
mostly though it is all in the hips
that's right it has shit all to do with wrists
and I have been practicing wrists for years
contemplating shitty advice
while I get jerked bone looseningly back and forth
I am never sure if I am angry
but there is froth in somebody's mouth
not about riding it out
about holding on
coming to terms with the flesh and blood of the bull that might throw me
that I have no idea where I would land

Day 3

Global warming causes "drunken" trees in Alaska
leaning over at unseemly angles from the earth
some "very drunk" have fallen over
the ground underneath them melted
moved from solid to liquid
not one day all at once
but slowly
steady climb of the days toward heat
they had broken foundations
then one day they noticed
and fell

The eighties are yelling at me from the TV
that "Marie realized she was only in relationships with losers"
in the land of the obvious made epiphany
you can after school special my relationships if you must
but thirty years have passed
since this passed for good advice
so I am just wishing us all
really good luck

I'm convinced!
easily
I am easily convinced
the push, the pull
tides of hope and fear perpetually washing my shore
waves strong enough to erode
I'm never sure how large I am
I never know the space I take up
fog thick
I trace circles inside myself ending up right back
ending up about to fall over tired
onto moist patches of grass
I wish I didn't recognize
I wish I understood better
could tell by the bend of the blades which way was east
so each day
I could make it to that part of myself to watch the sunrise

Day 6

there was a stretched out piece of myself
I couldn't quite reach the part that would give control
often felt like it was right there
like for sure I could reach it if I leaned over
I needed it
and my hands fell through the open air
fingers extended
expectant, out into the moment before I hit the
Roof
Bottle
Floor

Day 7

twist, twist
memories that feel like driving down a winding road through the forest
Too fast

Tiring night of chase my tail dreams
of headstand blown kisses
I remember thinking maybe I might
some actions feel dead
right in the middle of them you don't feel not feeling them
you walk in thinking buy one bottle of wine and walk out with three
you think well don't drink all three
I never remembered the end of the movie
must be because I fell asleep
must be

The hallway is lined with doors
on one side
windows on the other
not the kind of place you stand
walk through
walk back
with the frequency that feels like pacing
makes the place seem small
a few steps away
from everywhere I will go today
carpeted feeling of restless
drink the weak coffee for emphasis
still
don't want to go anywhere else
today

"The addict craves the absence of the craving state."

—Gabor Maté

Satisfy
    a)   meet the expectations of desires; comply with
    b)   be accepted by, as adequate; be equal to
I accepted
bottom of the bottle adequate
equal to whatever else was outside my door
I didn't want to crave, so much
that it is most of what I did
a fondness for the look of beer cans
the silhouette of wine bottles
mind clears right before the first swallow
mouth waters at the sound of freshly opened
wanting
there is no instance left behind by trauma
that could meet the expectations of desire
the gap between what you want and what happened
is too big

Kim

Halls don't set off breathalyzers
Your tour of this place was right after mine
empty leisure room, crowded caf
no laundry on move out days and when the hairdresser comes
this triage
line up out the door
will fill your spot as fast as they can
the birds are freaking out on the building across the alley
large clumps squawking and landing
then picking up and leaving again
there are hundreds of them

deeper we go
down into our self
searching for diamonds
the edges of the perfect problems buried
cut our hands
even if we wear gloves
even if we bring lamps
even if we have done this before
Still leave fingerprints in red on the earth as we try to climb out

emotions hit in waves
waves I am not watching
so like walls
smacking against my back
standing in the long reaching shallows staring at the shore
squint to make out what it is
past the beach
in the tall grass that is leaning over in the wind
straightening just to lean over again
whoever it is squints back
then it changes into a house that looks like it might not fall down
the waves keep hitting my back
smack, smack

Mixtures
little bit of
but mostly
yeah, it's better if you shake it
nothing goes with
like
you really have to try it
SO fucking good
but my favourite use to be
right after I
yep
you know what I mean

Day 15

Dreams on rooftops
really depend on how you feel about heights
Nightmares
about rivers in the dark
depend on how well you can swim
proximity of what you fear to what you love
reaches out and touches you on the shoulder
close enough you can hear the gentle tapping of its toe
toss the heavy feeling off
it lands back on me
weightier than before

Contribute
to what is hard to say
Add to the pile of things in the middle of the room that
no one will make eye contact with
our worst unkept secrets
then try your best
sweat, shake
like you are lifting weights
not judging
your own
mistakes on mistakes on mistakes

jumbled up notions
sharp edges
leave their marks on my mind every night
Addiction is a poem about a nightmare
Recovery is being aware you are writing a poem about a nightmare
Courage?
curled up inside myself mumbling
sweet dreams
staring at something I can't quite see
it's a hard to hold squint
scared of what I might see
scared of what I won't

I spread the ruins
read the cards
listen to the voice in the back of my mind
it is humming the theme song for *Dawson's Creek* though
cosmic busy signal
tomorrow then?
hopefully

Community Meeting

room full of people with some serious issues
raising concerns about less pressing matters
water left on the bathroom counter
whispers during self-help videos
little things
worth mentioning?
till
someone who wrestles with the beast they call bipolar
is shaking?

Laughing

weekend pass
our bed
always getting pulled out of
remember being pulled into
Remember falling asleep on her chest
remember Cooper's excited circles
claws sliding across the floor in ecstatic clamour
remember really good coffee
better conversation
Laughing
with her on our apartment floor
looking at me without my mask
joy is a tide rising in me
every time I remember
to remember

I was in Tofino thinking it was the most beautiful place I had ever been
simultaneously
thinking we didn't bring enough to drink
Not too much
so
not enough
We laid on the beach and watched a meteor shower
stars fell through the sky as waves crashed nearby
and I was thirsty
We walked the beach for hours and hours
made friends with starfish
and I was thirsty
We explored the little islands you can walk to when the tide goes out
talked through daydreams and layers of ourselves
and I was thirsty
I read to you my favourite fairy tale
propped up on driftwood, mist slowly receding off the ocean in front of us
and I was thirsty
I left you as soon as we got back
with no explanation
I was thirsty

So when does this become the much needed rest
someone said it was going to be?
I chase my thoughts around the room until I catch them
pin them down and tickle them
till I am laughing
This is a weird place to wake up
from someone who has woken up in some pretty strange places before
Before, I had no idea how I had gotten there
that was the strangest part
Now I know exactly how I got here
and that is by far the strangest part

Nervous #1

the feeling of right before the group is about to
but probably shouldn't
off to the races anyway
Except the race is between
a wheelbarrow full of water with a hole in the bottom of it
dripping
and a house that is trying its best to catch on fire
smoking
unsuccessful attempt, after attempt, after attempt

Go fetch me an altar
to a god I haven't met yet
I want to laugh at something sacred
or destroy something important
a thing drenched in meaning
that I don't for a second take seriously
Too much around here I am supposed to be gentle with
cupped hands and held breath
For fear I might break something of someone's
that is the only unbroken thing left

Full of yesterdays that destroyed me
standing at the front of the class
still not associating
I got an A minus on that presentation
so
Fuck the truck I destroyed
my dad bought it for himself for Christmas
for every year that I hate that holiday
for every time the sound of Christmas carols reminds me of screaming
I want to be
Done with pretending
done with protecting the people busy protecting themselves
so they can continue to leave thirteen-year-old me alone
to face down the drunken wrath of her mother

Unsure of my strength today
looking at the unlabelled box
hoping I can carry it to the door
hoping that if it is full of books they are about what I should do next
hoping this letter is addressed to the right future me
the one who will read it
the one who will stop right in the middle of
and
remember not to
the one who will make eye contact
with the versions of myself that I hate the most
and wink

Blacked Out

Probably better that way
my memory started to look like a loose-knit sweater
stretched
and I didn't give a shit
It helped before
took me somewhere safe
self-hatred smudges all over me
on parts even I can't see
it is not a place I went reluctantly
it is a place
I wanted to stay

Day 28

Weakness trading places with vulnerability
one not leaving willingly
the other not entering with any grace
neither acknowledging much
Tilted looks of shame dragged across their feet
I wish this set change had the curtain closed
or at least the audience would look away

The Twist

The dances we do with ourselves are elaborate
hard to watch
harder to interpret
impossible to imitate
Like snowflakes with factory defects
music all in separate heads
from different neighbourhoods
meals are on schedule
everything else feels a little less scripted

Haley

Next door, on the other side of the thin wall
is a young girl with a younger baby
she gets out today
into the chaos world of family, friends and strangers
Users
in all the places she knows where to find them
no help
in the fight to get her kid back
She can do the almost impossible with the rest of this
She could also get distracted
I will probably never know
but I will wonder
and hope

Iceland

Eight by eight picture of the ocean
done by a local artist
leaning beside my alarm clock
Massive waves pull me gently as I wake up
standing beside her
a calmness I am excited to feel
something I see when I look at the blue and the grey
when I remember trying to decide on a piece
getting distracted by her
my hand on her shoulder, sneaking a kiss in on her cheek
The photo feels enough like her to make the room feel like home

Chores

I want to tell her over the steam of the dish pit that the book on trauma
is great
but it's not
it could be about half as long and written better for the half that was left
There is some power in that
Isn't there?
Being able to talk about it, casually, while doing my chores
"he really didn't get it"
laugh together
wipe the counter and move on

Cross Contamination

That's what undoing compartmentalization feels like
straight through the middle of that swamp
Pretending I am challenging my fear of everything
by doing whatever I want
but
The cage isn't even locked
the first part isn't even over yet
my shoes don't even have laces that could come undone
Stand still for a second
a version of me premeditated?
or am I just hesitating?

hard to think of one day
standing in today
counting moments
till I get to talk to a lawyer
Grey thoughts
that haven't seen the sun in months
whisper "run"
I whisper back "fuck you"
I add the shitty milk to the shitty coffee
I wait to talk about it
Stay
to wait
to talk about it
even though I don't want to

Feels like someone took steel wool to my chest all night
breathing around the tangled mess that is left is a bit tricky
getting used to it though
little dance with my body to hold it together
The least I could do
The most anxiety could ask for
everyday begging to carry on
everyday an answer shaky
feet on floor?
feet on the floor

Lud Dub

In my mind
I am listening to your heartbeat
across this city
weaving its way through raindrops
The sound smells sweet
like your skin in the morning
It is the rhythm behind
all my movements that make sense
It is the sound that gives me the courage to listen

Friends

Ten-year-old me
standing outside the screaming house
always looks like it might fall over
Never does
I didn't want to go in
Learning how to stand there with her
to carry her on my shoulders
the hell out of there
The sun is coming up over the road to somewhere else
and we are on it

Used to days that feel like they sparkle and pop
Gunshots
off I go
onto
the same
left behind to the fuzzy haze
Here
the feeling of my scarf on my skin
the damp taste of winter air in my mouth
the sound of a friend laughing
Wednesday I fell to the floor crying
I blew my nose in a t-shirt I found there
Saturday is just a day I realize I am fighting for my life and I want to live
washed the shirt
think I will wear it on Wednesday

When I put my finger on it
it hurts
I want to stay with the frothy yeses
But I need early morning meetings
where I say it out loud
one thing each day I am proud of
one thing I am grateful for
Give myself chances
right in front of me chances
to make choices
I am ready to live in

Wrong Bed Side Of

Grinding sensation like there is definitely something off in that joint
clicking noise when I move like something healed wrong
After the
and right before I
fall into everything that I sit on
Musical chair music
playing over opera thoughts
or just lament me all the way to lunch and tell me I better be hungry
Just off
most of the right pieces
sound a fraction of a second
faster than the picture

Make Rehab Great Again

A level of aggressive ignorance
that at first is surprising
intriguing even
Until you realize it is real
changes over
too horrifying
to make sure you lock the door behind you
Deadbolt, you are hoping will keep you alive
the man sitting across the breakfast table
Believes children should be kept in cages
if they are at the wrong place at the wrong colour
Take away choices over my own body
Make my wedding illegal
staring hatred down before seven thirty a.m.
wakes me right up

Julie

You lasted three days
I met you twice
I don't understand why people don't stay
Your eyes had layers and layers of shields
different colours and shapes
I could see them moving when others would speak
You tried to open up
even through your doors were rusted shut or broken off
You said you missed home
"and it was fucked"
because home was your dealer's house
I think I know
where you are now
where you went, when you slipped out the back door
I wish I said more than just welcome
small talk here is absurd

Dig the sleep out of my eyes with a shovel
self-made hell
still
You can find a neighbour to borrow some sugar from
to build a fence
or start a rumour
to piss you off for a decade
be forgotten for another
You can find a friend whose hate matches up with yours
like you have the same shadow
you can march around ready for that fight
It will still surprise you
when the currents of anger sweep away the parts you were trying to keep

Triage

The morning cafeteria light is perfect
just like a hospital
The chair is exactly where I
sagging into its stiff uncomfortable
need to be
A place where a hundred thousand dollar
pending
insurance bill is small news
to pending cancer
and an amputated leg that is very much final
if not fully healed
Fourth party reeling with memories of her mother
something I know well
something I hope she gets away from somehow
Because I wish that for myself
to never again wake up from her screaming in my face
for our fourth to never again see herself reflected
one hundred times back at herself
in her mother's insect eyes

Day 45

Sound of her sleepy voice
coming through the pay phone mounted on the wall
Lights me up inside
she is in Seattle so the weather hasn't changed much
I will see her tomorrow
so I don't even have to wait lots
The hallway is filled with chaos
the whole building filled with jumbled pathos still frames
but I feel nothing but the sound of her voice

Tap-Dancer

Carve me out of someone else's soggy misbeliefs
I can tell you how to good posture
most of the way slumped over
how I always crave vanilla ice cream
But order double chocolate sea salt
I can makeup backwards
trusting in forwards
until we are all the way around that block
Till the gap between my stories
has gotten big enough from an awkward silence to fall through
land on something familiar
that we both don't recognize

Tweed

Not enough impossible to stop me from trying
I did exist
I was there
my father marked it on a map somewhere
tucked away
my mother took a picture that made its way into a frame
that's how you might know
there is a creek I fell into
there is a game I used to love to play
I happened to that place
whether it was okay with it or not
I got lost in its forests
I danced in its halls
I walked along its rivers
and graduated from its classes
I managed to leave
That last bit
is still my favourite thing about the place

Emma

You have the same name as my sister
and I had it in my head that we would get close over time
that we would go snowshoeing
that I would get to know a version of you less anxious
Friendship scares the movement out of me
back in a childhood where it wasn't safe to be seen
I never got the hang of it
but I wish
I could recognize your laugh from across the room
I hope you don't drive around those cliffs near your house
on the nights you don't remember
the rocks at the bottom are unforgiving
                                    even though we are sorry

The cracks in the paint on the wall of my childhood always took on shapes
a crane
a twisted tree
a river
Centipedes would crawl across the cracks while I was peeing
I would scream
but I couldn't run
Dirt floor basements
can't hardly blame them
that every one of their thousands of legs wanted to be close to our furnace
in the winter
I wonder if they were just as disconcerted as us
when on occasion the oil ran out
Cold creeping in from all the edges
I wonder if it killed any of them

Jailbird

Singing me songs about things I don't want to know
the people and places don't sound familiar
but oh the rhythm
That rhythm I know
it takes on a funny texture when it gets tangled in me
strikes against my mind like a match
lights my smirk
Gets me thinking when I shouldn't be
gets me places that I never have to try hard to go
I would whistle along but I find other things are on my mind
that trapped song somehow always leads me to other things

Blake

He died
I didn't know him well
but I remember him laughing
Uncontrollably
with her
the kind of laughter that bubbles up
Every time you think of the joke
they laughed for two days
I was scared of his laugh
afraid he was laughing at me
I wish he was here to laugh at this now
I wish I hadn't been scared of his joy
It was so badly needed
and still, it wasn't enough

Caving

In the woods I was camping in
last summer
there is a huge cave they found
Accidentally
by helicopter
while they were looking for caribou
it is the size of a soccer field going nearly straight down
The caribou want nothing to do with it
some humans can't believe they didn't know it was there
but I can

Berries

Juniper bushes grow in rocky fields
they are not much to look at
they are hell to walk through
But tough enough to suck water out of rocks
I think about it all the time
the really hard stuff I am supposed to grow from
Juniper bushes stay green through the snow and the cold
through the sun and the heat
steadiness
forcefully foster it in me

Body

getting me most of the way right now
hands and feet and eyes
Clapping and stomping and winking
like they always have
Grinding and leaking and wanting
like they always will
Flawless habit of shamelessness
sometimes
at the right moment in the evening and not before it

Nervous #2

So scared to do things that are for myself
that before family day
where it was my turn to speak
I shit myself a little bit
barely even noticed
just hopped in the shower and washed it off
I don't seem to register the different levels of fear
terrified
mild Anxiety
scared
alert
all the same
me trying not to look
I go blank
hope no one else will notice if I don't

Rory

"Bunch of fucking cunts
I fucking hate this place"
I tap on her door gently
but
still loud enough she would hear
there is more sobbing from inside
I knock once more
"Just shoot me in the head"
I can hear her storming around in the small space
she doesn't come anywhere near the door somehow
I wait there a moment
then walk down the hall
her swearing, raging and crying get softer with the distance
I half wish she had opened the door
Not usually this helpful
I just wanted to tell her
I hate it here too
sometimes
I hope she cries herself to sleep before she runs away

Crossless? Build One.

To the martyr with the shifty eyes
is your hard done by actually done by you?
is the making sure that it is not all that great
the wire underneath the papier mâché of your everyday life
Little closed loops built into our personalities
the fucked up way we pick out groceries
Stems from a time when we had to
twist ourselves around what was happening
to fit
to survive
now our thoughts sometimes move our hands in strange ways
Don't say that we don't make sense because we do
because we did

Day 58

China Shop Bull Blues

I would like my emotions to do what I tell them to do
same story from the other side of that fence
Not supposed to compromise
someone said
so this might take some time
I have it though
for myself
more than just crying on the floor of the shower
until it goes away
sit and listen to myself
A change in the world around me
started from holding the scared child within me
gently

If I turn myself into a rabbit and hop out of this hat
is it just another one of my tricks?
just a game I play with the mirror
Where I look like this
and then I look like that
if I do the things I don't want to
will it make me better at them
the important change is somewhere else
somewhere plain sight hidden
right beside believing I am good enough
so I can start to want to be different

Good luck and bad luck
are shifting around
On the same side of the same coin
the other side is the hot breath of addiction
washing away choice
Something comes along and flicks it
sends it spinning across the grains of the wooden tabletop of my life
someone whispers a bet
I don't disagree
but I don't venture a guess

Day 61

Made sense
I made it make sense
I gave the fire truck shape to the cloud
and it was shaped a bit like a fire truck
but it was never going to put this fire out
never going to get me to climb down from this tree
Took the language that the instructions were yelled in
and translated it into words that could be said calmly
Accent so thick
I use it for a diving board
so I could plunge right into deeper meanings
so thick that when anyone talks anywhere now
I can understand it
I use it as a lever to lift ten times my weight
well over my head
but I still can't stand the sound of it
The space it takes up in me makes me want to rip myself to shreds
start over
make myself make sense again

Hanged man's problem of swinging
I am
and I am not
and then I am again
Feet on the ground they tell me
always been distrustful of advice
still I listen
still it sways me
I touch the invisible edges of how far my weight will take me
Close
never satisfied with how far I get
I am a pendulum again and again for further than that

Difficult
Is so hard to tell
I couldn't say whether it is trying or impossible
but if I can do it right now for a moment
That is the proof I use to say
I can do it for another

Out of Water

The depth of the air in the sky is unimaginable to a fish
not because fish are unimaginative
because the sky near the top of the mountain's peak
can be guessed at
But open air
nothing for miles and miles and miles
but wind
is something you have to be very imaginative to see
even when you get to look right at it

Went full Jackson Pollock
on the game of Pictionary I was playing
with a room full of people
who didn't know I was hoping they would understand
still
sad no one guessed it
seemed so obvious to me

Shallow water drownings
not as interesting as scuba divers who run out of air
not as sad as infants who fell in the pool
still a way to die
a means to an end

Two A.M. Shower

Freedom is not a wish list
it's a chance you might have to take
I wanted to be clean
something I have always found hard to achieve
Apartment empty
dog unaffected by my whimsy
"What are you going to do when you get out of here?"
question I can't shrug at
Fight the "whatever I want" answer
trying to crawl its way out of my mouth
I won't
I will find little bits of pure freedom
and weave them into my new sense of meaning

Living with the kind of folks who try
extra hard to remember December birthdays
who make sure those guys get cards
In the same group one signs with a hateful remark
"dyke!" "queer!"
words
that still make me a little bit afraid for my life
His idea of a joke
groups are just individuals
things in common, things not
that guy got kicked out
I really hope he doesn't use
if he does I hope he doesn't die
Also that his friends, that I live with, didn't hate me
they would unwittingly
demonstrate why it is never just a joke to me

Question Marks

What if I can't?
What if three weeks go by and I leave here
more messy than I came?
What if I am the horror story?
What if I hit the bar on the way home?
People in this room aren't going to make it
am I one of them?
Mind drifts over that bleak desert-like thought
to land in an oasis
that statistics quickly take away
but for just a second
I wonder
Has the room ever held a group that entirely got sober?
that stayed that way
Could this be that group?
sandstorm of laughter
from a part of myself almost crying
No, not likely

Give me the grains from that hourglass
I will sprinkle them into the ocean at night
Wish I could say I knew the spell that it casts
sure that all magic is kinda like this
falling forward onto itself like the waves at my feet
Gentle prayers
talk with something greater than myself
feels like resting
Like being out of breath and knowing that there is more air

The underlying question
turns out to be when's lunch?
Humans are of two worlds
the physical and the physical
one far more complicated than the other
Don't put your feet up on the table
something I always remember if the table is nice enough
if the girl sitting at it is cute enough
if I am not distracted by thoughts that seem more interesting
if I am hungry

Bouncy

I want to take dance lessons
Right now
trampoline dive into a cool lake
when it is midsummer hot
Not once but seven thousand times
loudest, biggest, brightest
I see you Friday thoughts
I see you wiggle around in not enough
I see you fussing over perfection edges
building a story I can topple off of
Take you
morning energies electric tingle
jump into the crisp lake once or twice
Rest and let the sun dry the water on my skin
while the well-disguised fever
passes

Hassan

Parties kaleidoscope with options for self-distortion
friends see a difference where there really isn't one
because they couldn't be more proud of him
Ignorance is deadly when you are walking through the jungle at night
forget the tiger
if you lean on the wrong tree you might get one nasty parasite
He is gone
right before he could graduate
I am struck with the size of the void space where understanding needed to sit
I can see his father on family day
saying earnestly, "I hope that everyone does well here. That everyone is ok."

Gifts

There is a kid excited about her new sled
somewhere in here
I think I have got to find her
need her today
as much as she needs me tomorrow
when her brother runs into that sled
and breaks it

Over the Top

Not like the trenches
like my favourite kind of dress rehearsal
try to be too much for the stage
when nothing is too much for the stage
Going back to rehab
on Sunday evening
always thinking
I have an understanding of chaos
because I don't wear a watch
because allowing confusion comes naturally to me
because there is something comforting about the destructive nature of
change
because I don't understand it at all
because that is part of it
A spool fully unwound always just beginning to tangle

This Place

Always a guy in the cafeteria
wanting to prove to himself that he is powerful
by making people uncomfortable
by talking about how "men are"
like they don't have a choice
like he doesn't have a choice
When he can't stop talking about the tank top she was wearing
rules around clothing selective as usual
Stakes higher
good old traditional sexism
unmoved

Two Weeks

Pull me out of the oven prayers
to mountains
always listening
Never saying a damn thing
can I go home now
the dog
and the love of my life
Miss me

Living Room

Nearly everywhere is far away from here
that is just kind of how we think of places
spaced out
Wouldn't it be strange though
to have the living room follow you around
so that every room you were in
at any moment could feel like it
Familiar enough for me to try and sit on the couch that's not there
to not walk over the spot most likely to give me a sliver
uncomfortable overlay
There is a noise somewhere in a memory I can't quite hear
this is just a waiting room
or a friend's house
or an office building
It is also that damn living room
and I hated it there
I was terrified

Day 79

I want to capture butterflies and interrogate them
about what it was like to suddenly know they could fly
Ask them for the perfect metaphor
so I might know how it felt the first time they spread their wings
fearful confusion?
daunted and clumsy?
confident excitement?
as though they always knew
that having them meant knowing them
I am not sure but I think they would laugh
Then
I would have to let them go

Caution Thoughts

Association minefields
learn how to walk through them
mindful
Learn to pull yourself back out of that river
again and again if you have to
till the calluses on your hands are blisters
keep pulling
You can't afford to go there
this river leads to an ocean
that won't even notice when you drown

Louder

If it is late at night and you are all alone
most people play the violin
Not the fiddle
but I like the ruckus
If you have every light in the house on and the music blaring
it is hard to hear the ghosts
it is hard to see them
especially if you don't look

Not supposed to say things that make your counsellor cry
it is not a one-way street
but still
a dirt road
a polite, honour system firmly in place
Move the fuck over
or one of us is going off the road
I wasn't wrong to say what I said
but I am still looking around in it
for a gentler way

I don't always get me
which makes other people hard to understand
They are like hieroglyphs, under vines, on the temple wall
that's on the other side of the sign that says Do Not Climb
and they shoot people here for doing things they are not supposed to
But I have got to know
I can't live without them
looking into the eyes of a stranger
there has to be some recognition

Breathe out the complicated confusion
that is everyone's best guess
forget the gas can in my mother's hand
that place would have gone up like it had never heard the word insurance
I wouldn't blame her
but I was there
someone else
would think outrage
but they couldn't out rage us
they would say it wasn't her house
but they would say it wasn't my house
more than one hundred years old
what do they know about years in that place?
what do they know about what it costs to rebuild?
how did they not notice that her hands trembled?
that she cried
that she didn't do it
that he wouldn't have even noticed if the neighbours
hadn't stayed nosy all these years

Jumbling around for my new place in the world
Goldilocks the shit out of it
somewhere just right
Familiar
was a pile of necessary parts
to machines long ago thrown out
Familiar was something someone probably said
under their breath
so it couldn't be both those things
Safe and safe
puzzled, I am ripping the stickers off the Rubik's cube
reinvention is all in the blink
In the faith that there is a chance
and it might look like this

Comfy bed
careful resting
like I might break it
if I move too fast
if the parchment paper that is my peacefulness is thin enough
it will rip
I will fall through sweat soaked, twisted sheets
to sitting in every position this room has to offer
and two that it won't
because I just can't
for thirty minutes at a time
irregular intervals
but I might just land back in bed by morning

She said it is nice to hear my little voice
that I sound happy
but that I always sound happy
even if I am not
wonder where that comes from?
She sounds sincerely confused
worried
even though at twelve she found out I wanted to kill myself
She just called me selfish
and never spoke of it again

Vancouver winter morning
dark and wet
Skytrain screeching secrets meant to be whispered
feels better this way
with the crows' consistent irritated response
Puddles getting ready for the days rain
I have always loved the sound of trains
this morning I overflow for them
conjuring adventure
going somewhere
Sounds like a goddess licking her thumb to turn my page

Charlie

When she said she was standing on that bridge
I should have said
how glad I was that she didn't jump
I did say that she was looking good
She did say that she was feeling better now
feeling strong
Can't we just carry each other around?
to make sure that we are safe
I want to know that she is safe
little pieces of my heart wandering around this city drunk and high
I wish it was enough to stop them from hurting themselves
I wish it was enough to stop me from hurting myself

Release

Relief like ecstasy
not the drug
but the feeling
So kind of like the drug
all the moments that I just couldn't
and then did
Gives me a warm place to rest while I collect my thoughts
warm like a plant getting enough sun
Strong
when I leave
shocked I could do such a thing
Sit down
listen and intentionally change my life
Three months
is a lot of time
a lot to walk away from quietly skipping inside

Notes

"Day 3" was previously published in *Open Minds Quarterly*, 21:4, Winter 2020

"Day 10" borrows the line "The addict craves the absence of the craving state" from *In the Realm of Hungry Ghosts: Close Encounters with Addiction* by Gabor Maté (Vintage Canada, 1997)

"Day 24" and "Day 61" were previously published in *Existere Journal of Arts and Literature*, 39:1, Fall 2020

ANDREW ROWAT PHOTO

ASH WINTERS is an emerging Toronto-based poet. Queer and sober, their work navigates the intersections of addiction, identity, and trauma. Growing up queer in small town Ontario gave Ash a chance to develop a lavish sense of humour and a deep respect for empathy, both of which come through in their work. They graduated with their BA in English from Lakehead University in 2010. Their poetry has recently appeared in *Existere* and *Open Minds Quarterly*. *Run Riot* is their first book of poetry.